Tails of War
presents…

Barney

the Saga of a Paratrooper Dog in WWII

Story by: *Diane Condon-Boutier*

Illustrations by: *Elisabeth Gontier*

Other titles in the series Tails of War:

Spooky: the Adventures of a Ship's Cat in WWII
Zip: the Story of a Carrier Pigeon in WWII
Calliope: the Tale of a Police Horse During the Blitz

Other works by Diane Condon-Boutier:
Through These Doors; the Manoir at Bout l'Abbé
(a historical fiction novel for adults)

Barney: the Saga of a Paratrooper Dog in WWII

Copyright © 2019 by Diane Condon-Boutier

All Rights Reserved

Printed in France

No part of this publication may be reproduced, stored in or introduced into a retrieval system or transmitted, in any form or by any means (electronic, mechanical, photocopying, recording or otherwise), without the prior written permission of both the copyright owner and the publisher of this book.

The scanning, uploading and distribution of this book via the internet or via any other means without the permission of the publisher and the copyright owner is illegal and punishable by law. Please purchase only authorized electronic editions and do not participate in, or encourage electronic piracy of copyrighted materials. Your support of author's rights is appreciated

For my sister, Peggy - my rock and so much more than just a sister - who for many, long and happy years enjoyed the company of a brilliant border collie named Bubba...

"Grand-sire? How come you have a limp?" asks a pup so young he still regularly trips over his own feet and those of his littermates.

"Well, little fellow, it's a long story," I say, while stretching out my front paws and easing my bad leg out from under my body, shifting into a more comfortable position.

"Please tell!" yip his brothers and sisters. Soon, an entire litter of my descendants jostles into place in front of me and I lift my greying nose to the sky, remembering.

"It's a *very* long story, so you'll have to be quiet."

"We promise! Please, Grand-Dog! Tell us what happened!"

"Alright, because it was such a long time ago, I'll have to think where to start…"

****

You know I have a name other than 'Grand-Dog', that my real name is Barney and that I am a collie. But I wasn't always a family pet. I was born a shepherd - a working dog.

A shepherd's job is to ensure the safety of a herd of animals: to assemble them and protect them from attacks by predators. It's an everyday activity for a shepherd dog: living on a farm and moving sheep or cows from barn to pasture.

I'm retired now and spend most of my days dozing in the shade at the edge of the porch while my son's pups roll in the grass, chasing bugs and butterflies.

What's unusual about me is that I spent my working life NOT guarding animals. Instead, I protected humans: soldiers who flew off into Nazi-held territory in Normandy during the 2nd World War.

So, how did I land this important job?

I was born years ago on a farm in the middle of the quiet English countryside. My mother was a skilled farm dog, tending a large herd of sheep. I am one of a litter of five pups: with three brothers and one sister. One of the male pups was kept behind on our farm to help our mother with her work.

When we were four months old, the rest of us were donated to the British Government to train to become soldier dogs. We said goodbye, each going off into different branches of service and each attached to one special human who would work with us, day and night, from then on.

My trainer was called William. He and I knew each other so well that we could understand what the other was thinking without speaking aloud. William learned hand signals to communicate orders to me, and I learned different postures to communicate information to him.

For example, when I crouch low to the ground that means there's danger ahead: a stranger or an enemy of some kind, and William knows to be very careful.

I have a particularly sensitive nose. Smells are to me much like road signs with place names printed on them are to humans. Instead of reading the signs with my eyes, I read them with my nose. Each smell is unique. Every living being has its own very complex odor. I can remember and identify about a thousand different ones.

Some smells I associate with names. William has a wonderful smell: quite like a mixture of sun-warmed field grass and toasted bread. I love his smell most of all, because he's my special friend. I can sniff him far away, even if I can't see him and I'll run as long as it takes to reach him. I'm happiest when I'm by his side and I'm eager to watch his every move, listening with every fiber of my body to do as he requests.

I nap when he does, curled up by his side. I eat when he does, often sharing bits of his meal. I wash when he does, swimming in lakes and rivers before grooming ourselves afterward. We train for endurance together. When William runs, I run. When William walks, I walk. When he crawls, I crawl and when he jumps, I jump alongside him. I don't much like when he climbs high up into trees, because try as I might, I cannot climb trees. Still, I can jump onto low branches and I've shown him that I can balance very well and hide myself in the leaves.

William and I learned about explosives. He taught me to carry and deposit a package with a string on it, and then run away as fast as I can. When I'm safely away, he pushes the plunger on the detonator and a huge blast destroys everything around the package.

We have also learned how to detect explosive devices, buried in the ground by the enemy intending to do harm. One day, an officer came into our training yard with several kinds of exploding mines used by Nazi soldiers in occupied Europe.

Ordinary mines look something like tin cans of vegetables with three metal sticks coming out of the top. The sticks are the trigger wires. The Nazi soldiers hide the mines in the sand on the beaches of Europe and in the dirt along roads leading to hidden gun positions. If someone accidentally bumps one of the trigger wires, the explosive device goes off, leaving behind a huge hole in the ground. Everything close by is blown to bits.

In order to stay safe, when William and the other soldiers walk along a road, they use a metal detector. This looks like a long-handled frying pan. They sweep the path ahead of them searching for any buried metal. If the metal detector finds something, it makes a clicking sound and everyone stops in their tracks until the dangerous device can be dug up and neutralized.

Just to make things more difficult for us, Nazi engineers invented a new type of mine made of glass or wood. True to its name, a metal detector doesn't make a noise when it encounters glass or wood. So, the only way to find those kinds of mines, is for me to smell the explosive material hidden inside and alert William.

This part of my job is by far the most dangerous.

I have overheard sad stories about terrible accidents involving dogs who become too excited and who forget how serious this job truly is. Just a single second of not paying attention to my nose can cost me my life. I have to keep focused and pay attention to each and every smell. My safety and the safety of those around me depends on me remembering my training and following it to the letter. It's particularly important to me, because I worked alongside some of those dogs who forgot.

I can guess that you're thinking I should have gone back to the farm and spent a quiet life herding sheep. But I'm loyal to William and would do anything to keep him safe. That's my job.

And so, I follow his Majesty, the King of England's advice: 'Keep Calm and Carry On'.

****

One evening, I'm with William and his friends at an airfield. An entire squadron of planes is parked on the tarmac and we approach one of them. It's a Dakota C-47.

Piles of equipment are scattered all over the ground and our boys line up to pick up packets of supplies. They're dressed in flight suits with parachute packs on their backs. They've got quite a lot of gear attached to their shoulders and sides, khaki canvas bags tied to their legs and around their waists. When they finish piling on all those packs, they look rather silly since they can barely walk straight.

I'm feeling pretty nervous and show it by circling around William, while his friend Anthony hooks clips and fastens buckles onto William. I'm not sure what I should be doing in all of this hubbub. I just hope William isn't intending to leave me behind. I don't like being locked into the kennel when he goes off without me for special training.

William turns to Anthony and checks all of his friend's fastenings.

"What's this big bundle you're carrying?" William pats a large lump in Anthony's rucksack.

"Just something extra I thought I'd bring along, in case we needed it," Anthony's got a shy smile and clearly, he doesn't want to tell what's in his bag.

"Alright then, keep your secrets! Up you go!" William helps push Anthony through the back door of the plane. "You'd think you were weighted down enough without dragging personal items along! But, it's your business after all!" William laughs.

The motors begin to chug and shake as the plane comes to life. The propellers slowly start to turn as the engine rumbling grows. Other planes on the smooth tarmac of the airfield begin to move, some of them going faster and faster before lifting off the ground and taking flight. The intensity of the noise bothers me and I bark and run in frantic circles around William's legs. I almost wish he'd take me back to the kennel away from this racket!

He pulls himself over the ledge and into the back of the Dakota already carrying Anthony and a group of men I know very well. The rest of our mates climb inside. There goes Ethan and Danny and Ryan and Colum, Edward and Harry and Michael and Billy. More smells and more boys, all friends. And they're leaving me behind?

Drat! That's a worse feeling than when William climbs a tree! He's going without me! Leaving me stranded here on the tarmac, while he and his friends drive away!

The plane shakes and several friendly faces appear in the door frame surrounding William. I crouch and bark at him. I'm wagging my tail hard, signaling that he's forgotten something very important: ME!

'What are you thinking, leaving me behind?' I'm frantically barking and jumping before crouching to let him know it's dangerous to leave without me.

Slowly, those big wheels begin to turn. I can see the soldiers laughing and talking to William, pointing in my direction. I'm alert and watching closely, waiting for William to signal to me. The plane is moving away and I follow alongside, jumping and barking and crouching. The wheels turn faster and faster.

Finally, there it is! The hand signal from William to come to him just as the plane begins to pick up speed. I strike out at a dead run. The boys all cheer when I take one easy leap through the door as the plane rumbles down the strip. We all fall back onto the floor of the plane, the boys laughing as I leap onto each one in turn, licking their faces with joy.

I am relieved to be along for the ride. They take seats along the sides of the plane just as we feel the engines shudder and we lift off the ground. We're climbing into the sky! Flying isn't like anything I've ever felt before! But as long as I'm with William, everything is fine.

****

"Grand-dog! You flew into the sky? Like a bird?"

"Yes, I did. Just like a bird. A very noisy bird. But we flew and flew and flew all across England and down to the coast of the English Channel."

"Wow!" yip the pups, squirming in excitement. "Grandpa flew like a bird!"

"Sometimes we were very high and everything we saw from up there was very small. Cows in the fields were tiny specks of brown and houses were little squares. All around us were other planes and when the sun dropped out of the sky and night fell, the full moon shone on the wings of an entire flock of airplanes. But what I remember most about that flight was when we crossed through the clouds hanging over the waters of the English Channel. The wind made a lot of noise...but I was ready, because I'd trained for this."

****

"Come here boy, time to get you suited up!" William has finished his mug of tea and the boys are packing up the rest of the sandwiches they've been sharing during the flight. I stop to snatch up a fallen triangle of bread spread with gooseberry jam. I don't much care for gooseberry jam but I swallow it anyway because I'm hungry and like before all of our practice jumps, I've not been given any of their food.

William and Colum are unfolding my harness and laying out the straps.

I sit quietly at William's feet, waiting for him to slip my front paws through the loops. There's a pack attached to the top of my harness with a clip and a strap on it. It feels heavy and uncomfortable so I squirm around a bit.

"He doesn't much care for this, our Barney," says Colum with his Scot's accent.

He's right. I don't really like jumping but I know there's a piece of steak waiting for me on the ground. I can smell it in William's pocket.

"Ready now boys! We're approaching our target zone!"

The boys begin shifting on their seats, anxious to go, waiting for the lights on the dial near the back door to change from red to green.

"Stand up! Hook up! Equipment check!" the order is shouted and immediately the boys reach to the ceiling, clipping their straps to the cable running the length of the plane.

William clips mine on just behind his own.

The lights turn green, and the jumpmaster shouts "Go! Go! Go!" One by one they're out the door with a swing of the leg and a jaunty twirl in the air as the strap attached to the rip cord snaps, and the huge sheets unfold.

William is out the door and I stand barking at the exit. He turns to look back at me, beckoning with the familiar hand gesture and I leap out into the air.

No, I don't like jumping at all.

****

But here I am falling through the sky, farm fields rushing up to catch me, treetops looming ahead in the dark.

I crash through some bushes and am a little dazed. My harness and parachute are tangled in branches and my feet are dangling just a bit off the ground. I let out a yelp of distress.

In just a minute, William finds me and holding me under one arm, he begins slicing through the cords attaching me to the tangled chute. I can smell the steak in his pocket.

Free at last! He gestures to me to sit, not using any words. Quietly, he unwraps the piece of meat and hands it over. By the time he's folded the paper and stuffed it in his pocket, I've finished and am licking my chops.

William squats in front of me and runs both hands from my muzzle along my ears and down the sides of my body. I stand and he runs a hand over each of my legs. I'm waiting for his next command.

I can feel his excitement. His body is giving off that unique smell when he's scared and excited all at once. It makes my muscles quiver, ready to run.

"Round 'em up, boy!" he whispers in my ear, and I'm off.

****

This is unfamiliar territory. I heard the boys talking during our flight. They mentioned Normandy. That's in France!

All I can think is that this Normandy place smells wet. The ground beneath my paws is kind of squishy and swampy. England doesn't feel like this except when it rains for weeks on end through the winter. Still, my nose is busy seeking out the smells of the seventeen boys I'm meant to assemble.

Colum is first, straight ahead of my nose. As we cross a field together, I sniff out a boy hidden here and there. Each one of them seems very happy to see me. A group forms, following my lead.

I'm the leader of this pack because while I'm searching out my boys, I'm also paying close attention to the ground ahead of us.

At the edge of the field I drop to a crouch. A familiar smell sets off a warning in my brain.

DANGER! I smell explosive material.

William puts his hand on my nose to indicate that I shouldn't bark out a warning message. Tonight, we must keep as quiet as possible since we are in enemy held territory. A Nazi soldier might be close by.

William and I stay still. Hand signals are passed along the line behind us, transmitting the warning from one boy to the next. When the message reaches Ryan, he moves to the front of our line to replace William. With Ryan's hand on my back, we inch forward until the smell becomes so strong that I know the mine is directly in our path.

This time I press my belly flat to the ground and don't move a whisker. It's right there, a mine canister with three trigger wires just inches from my nose!

Ryan unhooks a small shovel, called an entrenching tool from his belt and begins gently digging a shallow trench about a foot away from the mine.

On ordinary days he might finish the job by digging it right out and flinging it far away from us. But that would cause a big explosion and even if it would be at a safe distance from us, it would still make a lot of noise. Tonight, we can't risk attracting the attention of the Nazi soldiers who planted this mine. So, we leave it unexploded, but place a marker by it so that other boys don't fall into this deadly trap.

Our little column of paratroopers carefully steps around the marked-out mine and Ryan and Edward begin to climb up a steep embankment planted with a line of trees on top. The brush between the trees is very thick and filled with brambles. Tiny buds of blackberries dress the thorny branches. Later this summer, this hedgerow will be filled with fruit. I imagine local children will be picking buckets-full to bring home for jam making. But for now, the brambles are a painful nuisance, slowing us down as they tear at our fur and clothing. From the back of our line a pair of wire clippers appears to help cut a path through the stubborn thorns.

Edward and Ryan gently slide down the other side of the embankment directly into a sunken lane. Facing them is yet another embankment, and I can hear noises in the field behind it.

I stop still and crouch my front legs to the ground. I need to let William know that something is behind that embankment…something or someone!

The boys gather onto the track leading to our left and right between the hedgerows. Billy looks at his compass, holding it into a small patch of light filtering down through the leafy oak trees planted on top of each ridge. A full moon finally breaks through the clouds, allowing a milky glow to kiss the ground. There's just enough light to for Billy to read the dial and choose our direction.

We've been trying to replicate the path the Dakota was taking as it dropped us out the back door. Our boys should have fallen more or less in a straight line over about two miles. If we can stick to the flight path, we should be able to pick up our boys one after another just as we'd done up until now. That means we can't take the lane; we've got to cross the fields, breaking our way through the hedgerows surrounding each of the fields in Normandy.

And the field just ahead of us is occupied. But by who? Or what?

Harry moves to the front of our group, his rifle at the ready. He will be the first of us to engage the enemy. Slowly he inches his way up the smooth side of the embankment opposite us. The other boys crouch, laying themselves flat against the grassy side of the lane, guns primed and ready to protect Harry, should he need protecting. I can smell their fear and a quiver runs through me, lifting my fur. One of the boys pulls on a string around his neck, extracting a communication device from the inside of his jacket.

Gently he blows into the whistle. You can imagine my surprise when instead of a whistling sound, a loud 'QUACK!' comes out.

I can't believe my ears! It's a duck call! I can't help myself and let out a quiet 'woof!'

Suddenly, from the other side of the hedge, an answer rings out.

"Moooo!"

Harry pokes his head through the brush to look straight into the face of a very large spotted cow!

A herd of a dozen Norman dairy cows has gathered along the edge of a pasture. They must have heard our advance and come to greet us – our first welcome by locals!

All around, my boys breathe a sigh of relief and some of them can't stifle a quiet chuckle. They're all quite happy to have been met by four-legged locals rather than by the enemy!

****

The pups roll about in the dust laughing until their sides ache.

"Grand-dog met up with the locals, all right!"

"Local cows!"

"Yup! Not enemy Nazi cows, friendly French cows!"

"Did you get any milk for your tea, Grand-dog?"

I let them have their fun, teasing me about my first encounter on that famous day. Still, I remembered all too well that our amusement was to be short-lived.

"Nope! No fooling around taking milk and tea breaks, kids! We kept moving. We had a job to do before the sun came up, a mission to achieve in the dark..."

****

I set off at a run across the cow pasture, confident there will be no mines. Surely even Nazis wouldn't harm innocent cows!

I'm eager to link up with the remainder of our stick of eighteen soldiers. Along with the others, I've still got to find Vincent: our radio man and George: our medic.

These two boys are pretty much defenseless if they're all alone, because of the amount of heavy equipment they're carrying. There was no extra room for weapons when they jumped out of our plane. They don't have rifles to defend themselves if they run into the enemy.

Vincent is our communications link home. And George? Well, I'm hoping we won't need George's medical skills today, but better to have him around, just in case.

My nose is sniffing in all directions at the same time. So many unfamiliar smells! My brain is working hard to filter out the ones I must ignore; smells of night dew on flowers and field grasses, all smells I love but have to put aside to concentrate on the faint smells of the boys I'm searching for, like images of their faces floating toward my nose on the summer's night breeze.

Normally a dog would be delighted to romp through a strange pasture after dark, crossing paths with the creatures native to Normandy. I should be making the acquaintance of hedgehogs and rabbits, field mice and farm cats, owls and bats. It's hard to stay focused as they scurry though the lush French fields. I'd much prefer to follow their wild scents leading me on a merry chase through the night. Instead, I skid to a halt.

I smell a human! I smell cigarette smoke!

Raising my nose to the sky, I double check exactly what is wafting towards me. That's not a human I recognize, and the smell of that particular tobacco is unfamiliar as well.

Now, my ears begin to pick up voices. Not English voices. These voices are speaking in chopped tones that sound harsh and guttural.

Here comes a familiar odor of gun grease, too. So, they must be men with weapons. I'm afraid I've stumbled upon a group of enemy soldiers!

Should I turn and run back to warn William? Or go forward and find our missing men? Maybe it would be better to go make sure William is safe, first. What should I do?

Thinking hard, I decide that since he's sent me forward to search out George, Vincent and the rest of the boys, I'd better stay on track and proceed with my mission. I haven't got any more time to waste. If there are enemy soldiers on patrol, they could find my boys! I was trained to follow orders and that's what I've got to do! Fast!

At a full out run, I bolt directly into a group of uniformed men standing around chatting and smoking cigarettes. They're gathered around a large cannon on wheels, attached to a lorry.

They scatter and shout as I burst through their cluster. One of them falls as I crash headlong into his legs, knocking him over like the head-pin on a bowling lane.

"Yikes!" I yelp in pain as I roll head over tail, the breath knocked out of me. That hurt! I get one look at the soldier on the ground next to me and even though I don't understand his words, I'm sure they're not pleasant. I think he's cursing at me in German!

Other hands make a grab for my collar, trying to seize me by the scruff of my neck. I don't know those hands either.

I hate to do this. But I have no choice. If they catch me and trap me, I won't be able to complete my mission. Wriggling furiously, I turn my neck around in my own skin, allowing me to snap my teeth at those hands. A quick nip reaches skin and I can feel soft human flesh on my tongue. Yuck!

The hands let go, just as a boot kicks me in the side and I roll away yelping in pain. That hurt too, but at least I'm free and can make a run for it.

I'm running as fast as I possibly can though an empty field leading away from the Germans. A gun makes its loud 'CRACK!' as a bullet stirs the wind just by my ear. Another bullet thumps into the dirt behind my feet as I'm dashing cross-country towards the next hedgerow, looking for cover.

Yet another bullet, thumps just ahead of me, triggering a mine I'd forgotten to smell for. The ground explodes in front of my feet. Globs of dirt and chunks of turf fly into the air, then rain down over top of me, pelting my back and head. I can't see anything though this mess but I have to keep running.

The hedgerow is just ahead of me. I can smell bushes and trees and something metallic. I take a wild leap toward those smells and land in a mangled mass of barbed wire. Metal teeth bite through the fur on my face and chest.

"Yikes!" I yelp in pain again, forgetting to be quiet as I roll helplessly entangled in coiled razor wire. Panic sets in. I yelp and cry out, over and over again, forgetting my orders as the wire wraps itself around my legs and belly, digging in and trapping me.

"Barney!" a familiar voice whispers my name!

"It's our dog, Lieutenant!" Excited whispers come from the other side of the hedgerow.

I've found them!

Relief floods my brain. I've found the rest of my boys!

Familiar hands lift me out of the mess while other hands work quickly, clipping the rolls of barbed wire embedded in my fur. Little by little, it loosens its prickly hold on my skin.

But the enemy is just behind us. Worse yet, they're parked between William, leading the first group I've rounded up, and this second group led by the Lieutenant who's busy cutting me free.

****

The boys gather around me while conferring with the Lieutenant in hurried whispers. They heard the gunshots and the mine exploding. George-the-medic begins to swab the cuts on my face, ears and body left by the concertina wire. Disinfectant stings!

"Sir, do you reckon those Jerrys across the field know that Barney's a British service dog?" he asks the Lieutenant.

"They did see him running in this direction, they're bound to come looking for him" adds Harvey-the-bazooka operator.

"I don't think they'd chase down a dog. They're probably assuming he blew himself up when that mine went off. He looks just like one of the local shepherd dogs anyway. They'll be thinking he's a farm dog who got loose, chasing after a fox," says the Lieutenant.

I'm happy to believe him, and thump my tail in agreement.

"I hope you're right, Sir! I don't guess Jerry would wander through a mine field after a dog. Even if it is his own mine field! At least not until the sun's up, anyway."

"Even so, we should get moving, as dawn is only about an hour from now."

As George finishes examining me by running his hands over my legs and body one last time, the boys begin to hoist their guns onto their shoulders, making ready to set off once again.

"Hold up a minute, boys! We seem to be forgetting something. Barney's here with us, but where's William? He should be with Barney! That means there's part of our stick on the other side of those Germans."

"Well, we can't leave them behind, now can we?" says the Lieutenant. "That would be out of the question!" He bends over to pat me on the head, while speaking to George. "How is our dog, George? All right for another run, do you think?"

I'm pleased at the turn their conversation is making. For a minute, I thought they'd forgotten about my William!

"I guess he's alright, Sir. Shame our Barney can't talk, though," adds George. "It would be handy to know just how many Jerrys are over there! What do you have in mind, Lieutenant?"

I agree, thumping my tail against George's legs. If only I could share with them everything I saw, everything I know! The Germans have a cannon and these boys don't know it.

"Hey Lieutenant? Didn't William teach Barney to drop a package and run?" asks Harvey-bazooka.

"Well, yes. But William taught him the hand signal, not you, or me for that matter. Does anybody know what the signal is?"

Around the circle, all the heads shake no.

"Er, no, Sir. And a shame that is, Sir. I'd like to deliver some explosives right into the middle of their little camp and shake things up a bit!"

That sounds like a bad idea to me. No tail thumping coming from me after that dangerous remark.

"Wait a minute! Barney's collar! Remember? There's that space in the leather for messages. We can send him back to William carrying a message telling where we are, how many of us are here and warn our boys about those Germans stuck between us." Pockets are checked and a paper and pencil are produced.

The Lieutenant writes out a message assisted by an electric torch flashlight. Harvey and Vincent shelter him by holding an unfolded parachute above his head forming

a makeshift tent to help contain the beam of light in case any Nazi soldiers are patrolling within sight.

The light is switched off, the message rolled into a tiny tube shape. Vincent gently removes my collar and slips the rolled paper into the space hidden between the outer and inner layers of leather. Once my collar is fastened back around my neck, the Lieutenant kneels down to rub my ears and fur ruff.

"Barney, it's up to you, old boy! Watch out for mines in that field and steer clear of Jerry...but go find William!"

Those are the words I was waiting to hear. My body trembles with excitement as the Lieutenant leans over and plants a kiss on the top of my head.

I take a moment to return the favor with a quick face wash.

Wiggling happily as George gently lifts me over the remains of the concertina wire, I drop to the ground in the mine field, anxious to be off in search of William.

"Go with God!" I hear whispered through the brush behind me as I set off.

This time I've got to be more careful because I know the field could be planted everywhere with those deadly mines. Still, I have to hurry because the horizon behind me is starting to glow pink with the coming sunrise. Soon, the enemy will be able to see me!

****

Once again, I can't help thinking I should be enjoying myself. Nose to the ground, I'm retracing a path through a field which should be pasture land, feeding plump sheep or horses. Instead it has been turned into a danger zone filled with booby traps designed to kill. I have to wonder: who is more savage? Man, or beast? But I'm afraid I already know the answer to that question.

My path through the field is a zig-zag, avoiding the crater left behind by the exploded mine and skirting around the smells of other explosive devices primed to go off. As I approach the Germans and their artillery, my nose picks up the smell of more mines, these more closely spaced and I must slow my pace. I saw how powerful that device was and I have no desire to take a wrong step. If I don't make it out of this mine field alive, then William won't get the message I'm carrying and he might be in danger.

Quietly, placing each paw carefully as far away from the smell of explosives as possible, I pick my way towards the

Germans and their tobacco smells. They've brewed some coffee and the mix of smells masks the odor of the explosives. The smells pile up in my brain, cancelling each other out and I realize I have to be extra careful. The only path through the mines leads directly to the group of Germans.

This time I crouch close to the ground, trying not to be spotted by the coffee-drinking, cigarette-smoking German gun crew who appear to be engrossed in important discussion over a map.

As I'm hiding in the long grass, a strange vehicle approaches carrying two soldiers on an open back seat and one driver. It sounds like a motorcycle but looks like a tank propelled on treads instead of wheels. The driver stops and the passengers step off, handing over an envelope to the commander of the gun crew. It looks like it contains important news, maybe even announcing our arrival and the invasion from the sea that the Allies have been planning for months.

The Nazi soldier in command rips open the envelope and scans the contents before exclaiming *"Teufel! Sie kommen!"* As he turns to share the news with his comrades, I decide it's time to make my move.

With their heads bent over the paper, helmets almost touching in a circle, the Germans' attention is focused on one man holding vital news.

I make a mad dash just feet from the soldiers, leap to the top of the hedgerow and crash through the brambles. Behind me I hear their bolt-lock rifles engage bullets while shouting *"Was ist das?"*

They must have felt me rush by more than saw me, heard me thrash my way through the bushes. Bullets whiz blindly by me as I bolt across the cow pasture. I know my boys are on the other side of it, waiting for me.

By now, at the far end of the field, the entire herd of cows has gathered in a clump, giving away the spot where my boys have taken cover.

Cows, being curious creatures – particularly dairy cows who are used to being handled by humans – are compelled to investigate the arrival of anyone near their field. They'll eventually congregate closest to people, unlike beef cattle who have good reason to be wary of interaction with humans. Their intention to seek out human company was as effective as a blinking neon sign, pointing to where my boys were hiding. All I had to do was follow the cows.

I could only hope that none of those German soldiers behind me grew up on a dairy farm.

No mines in the cow pasture – luckily for the cows – means I waste no time crossing through. The cows are startled by my sudden appearance and when I let out a quiet 'woof!' greeting they canter off a few feet.

Harry pokes his head through the brush whispering "Barney? Is that you, boy?"

Almost immediately, I'm hoisted through the hole cut out in the blackberry branches, and hauled over the ridge into the sunken lane. At the same time the sun begins to peek through the trees bordering the field.

Elsewhere, just a few miles from our position, thousands of boats, hailing from a dozen different countries approach fifty miles of Norman shoreline. They're carrying a landing force of over a hundred and fifty thousand men preparing to push the Nazi army back to Germany. Today is June 6th, 1944. Today is D-Day.

****

I sit and scratch at my collar with my back paw. This draws attention to it and William immediately bends to remove my collar.

"Good boy, Barney! Lads, we've got a message!" Pats of congratulations at a job well done land all over my head and body.

"Drat! German soldiers are on the other side of that cow pasture! And on the other side of them, we'll be facing a mine field before we can reach the Lieutenant. He writes that the radio has been damaged, so we'll be going it alone without help from anybody else. He reminds us that we need to proceed southeast toward the town of Petitville, and that we need to at least join up with his group and the bazooka team in order to do that. We've got a river to cross and a bridge to take out before setting up our blockade! So, to help us reach the Lieutenant, they're going to launch an attack at the German squad from the east, drawing their attention towards the mine field. Which should allow us to sneak up from behind while they're looking the other way."

"Sounds like a lot on our plate, lads, but we have no choice. The longer we wait here on this lane, the more likely we'll be spotted by a German patrol." says Colum.

Everyone is thinking out loud, whispering at once and weighing out the best way to get across the cow field without being seen by the Germans on the other side.

"Well, we know the pasture isn't booby-trapped, so I think we should just crawl across it keeping our heads down," says Harry.

I thump my tail. It's true. No mines in that field. But there's a German cannon on the other side.

"Sun's on the rise, lads. It's now or never." The boys all nod at each other and I'm lifted into the pasture once again, followed by each boy, sheltered from sight by the cows.

William, Colum, Harry and the others lie flat on the ground and begin to squirm on their bellies across the field. I'm leading the way, crouching low to the ground, camouflaged by the long grass. The cows watch us wiggle away likc a herd of worms.

We're making nice progress through the field when the inevitable takes place. The boys are crawling through an area peppered with cow pies.

They're smelly and sticky and pretty nasty. I hear snorts of disgust from behind me, and wish I could take a moment to laugh, but our job is too serious.

"This is just perfect!" whispers Harry." The Nazis are going to smell us coming before they hear us coming!"

"Look at it this way, it's so gooey that it helps with camouflage. All you have to do is gather a few leaves and twigs, stick them to your chest and you'll pass yourself off as a bush!" jokes Colum.

"I could do with a cup of tea," murmurs someone along the line of squirming boys.

"Only you could think of food and drink at a time like this! You reek of cow poo! Doesn't the stench put you off your stomach?"

A whispered smattering of light-hearted banter hides their nerves, but I can smell the tension. It grows as we progress through the grass. We all fall silent as we approach the hedgerow opposite.

Suddenly, a huge explosion rings out from behind the embankment ahead of us. That must be Harvey and his bazooka!

Shouts and noises burst from the German gun crew. We can hear the clanking sounds of a big gun being loaded and primed. There's smoke and the smell of greenery on fire.

"Drat it all! They've got a cannon!" whispers Harry.

"Afraid so…and now it's being aimed at the Lieutenant! Let's go lads! Up and over!" shouts William.

Our group leaps to their feet and dashes the last yards to the hedgerow. Climbing up and over it, they surprise the German gunners who quickly turn around but don't have time to shoot their rifles. A hand to hand struggle between the two sides unfolds. I'm in the thick of the fist fight, snarling and snapping at any German uniforms I can reach.

It's over rather quickly, even though we don't outnumber them. A surprise effect has worked well for us this morning.

My boys end up with some cuts and a lot of bruises but not much worse than an ordinary pub brawl. The Germans are rounded up, disarmed and their hands tied behind their backs.

We've made a lot of noise, when our orders were to stay as quiet as possible. So, the boys begin working quickly to move away from this dangerous spot. While they're clearing up, William decides to make his way through the mine field behind me to gather the Lieutenant and the others.

I'm beginning to know this field so well by now that I barely move slower than a trot. In just minutes, we've safely crossed it and I'm yipping at the Lieutenant in greeting.

Much back slapping, hand shaking and congratulations meet us at the top of the hedgerow. "We've got them, sir!" announces William, "Six Jerrys and one of them's an officer!"

"Well, done! But what's that all over your jacket? And what's that smell?" asks the Lieutenant, wrinkling his nose with a grimacing frown. "But more important than your appearance, is there anything we need to retrieve from over there, William?" asks the Lieutenant.

"Well sir, there's a cannon! And some paperwork and maps that look important, Sir. And yes, sir, that's cow poo. I can explain, Sir…"

"Well no need for explanations, this is Normandy. Bound to be lots of cows. Just tell me the cow is fine, William, and let's have Barney lead us back across the field one more time to have a look at what Jerry's left for us."

"All of the cows are just fine, sir," laughs William.

That's how we ended up with a German cannon and a German truck and a pretty nifty German jack-rabbit half-track before breakfast on D-Day!

****

"Wow! Grand-Dog! You had a jack rabbit for breakfast?"

"Not one with fur, silly pup! A German half-track vehicle, with a motor-cycle front end is called a jack-rabbit. Probably because they're quick and can run through fields."

"Ohhhh! Not very tasty, I'll bet!"

"Ahhh. No." I'd forgotten how silly puppies could be.

"Shhhh! Be quiet, Sparky! We want to hear the rest of the story!"

"Yeah! Let Grand-Dog finish, Sparky!" yipped the other puppies, restless and impatient. They'd been listening to me for a good long while. I was surprised I still held their attention.

"Alright, alright! Let's see, where was I...?" I say, trying to pick-up where I'd left off.

"You were telling us about capturing a truck and a cannon!"

"That's right! Thank you! Now, we still had our mission to complete but at least we were grouped together and could make a plan..."

****

"If we follow the indications on this German map, we can avoid their gun positions and reach Petitville village from the north," says the Lieutenant.

"This lane doesn't seem to have any enemy defenses on it at all. We can use their lorry and get there in no-time!" says Harvey.

"Yes, but then again, we'll look like an enemy convoy if any of our own planes fly overhead. It's daylight. There's bomber support looking to take out gun positions and if we go driving around in Nazi vehicles, our fly-boys will think we're the enemy!"

Anthony pushes to the front of the group. "I've brought a Union Jack with me, lads! We can spread it over the roof of the lorry where the Germans can't see it, but our planes can!"

"Well now, that's a rather grand idea!" says the Lieutenant.

"Is that what the lump in your rucksack was?" asks William.

"I thought it might come in handy somewhere over here!" grins Anthony.

"Good thinking, mate! Hand it over and we'll tie it on the roof!" Sudden hope and enthusiasm flood the field and the overall mood of my boys lifts when the flag is shaken out and draped over the truck used to haul the cannon.

"If we had time I might burst into 'God Save the King!', but I guess we'd better stay quiet!"

"How about that cup of tea, now, Sir?"

"Private, I'm amazed that you can think about tea at such a time! But actually, that sounds quite nice. So, let's be quick about it, then off we go!" agrees the Lieutenant.

From every rucksack tin mugs appear, a tiny burner lights up and water is boiled, tea brewed and stirred with sugar and dried milk. Within five minutes everyone is sipping, and whispering  like boys on a camping trip. It's incredible what a cup of tea can do for the morale of an Englishman!

****

"Tea, Grand-Dog? Really? They took time out to make tea?" asks one of the pups.

"Yes, they did! And it was surprising what effect that cup of tea had on the spirits of my boys. They were almost happy."

"Happy to be in a war, Grand-Dog? How could that be?"

"No, I'd have to say that they were happy to be making progress in a fight against a military movement that was headed by such an awful person."

"Yeah, Adolph Hitler was the best bad guy ever!" pipes up one of the male pups.

"How can he be the best at anything?" asks one of the girls.

"Well, let's just say that Adolph Hitler, as the leader of the Nazi party had very few redeeming qualities, and leave it at that. It's a very good thing that his Third Reich did not last a thousand years as he said it would. This might be a very different place we're living in if the Allies hadn't been successful in crushing the Nazis," I explain. "The Second World War was probably the most important war in modern history."

"Tell us what happened next!"

"Well then, feeling a bit refreshed, we all climbed into the truck and three of our boys led the way on the jack-rabbit - not the furry kind! We set off down the sunken lane leading in the direction of Petitville to continue our mission…"

****

At first it was slow going only because we were cautious not to be intercepted by enemy troops.

But, at one point in time we chose to adapt our plan of action. We understood that driving quickly wouldn't give the Germans time to recognize the type of uniforms of the people using their vehicles. So, from then on, we drove at full speed.

Once we plowed right through the middle of a German patrol. They jumped so quickly out of the way, that I don't think they realized that it was Englishmen behind the wheel and not Germans.

News had clearly reached the Nazi army that the big invasion had begun. Everyone was on alert, but there was so much happening, and it was happening so fast, that we actually slipped through unnoticed. We charged through hamlets and crossroads at as high a speed as we could. Within about a half hour we could see signs for Petitville.

In order to complete our mission, we had to lay an explosive charge on the bridge in the center of town. I just hoped it wasn't going to be my job to drop the package.

"OK, lads! There's the village straight ahead of us. The main road leading through the town is a major route going east and west, used by the Germans to carry men and supplies in and out of this area. Behind us to the west, the invasion is unfolding and what we don't want is for the Germans to respond by moving a lot of extra soldiers into that zone. Our boys landing on the beach have enough fish to fry. It's our job to block the arrival of additional soldiers by taking out this bridge."

"The truck has gun shells in it for the cannon. Can't we just drive it up and leave it on the bridge?" suggests George.

"Leave it to the medic to determine what our plan should be!"

"No really, that's a great idea! That way, just a few men are in the thick of it. We'll drive onto the bridge, jump out and run. Then Harvey can take aim at the truck with the bazooka and blow it up."

"That won't blow up the bridge. But what it can do, is block the approach to the bridge on one side while one of us lays the charge under the bridge supports on the other side," replies Edward.

"You mean, use the truck explosion as a diversion while the explosive charge is placed under the bridge?"

"Colum, you're our explosives chap. If we drive you up close in the truck, how much time to you need to attach the charge on the bridge support?"

"Just a few minutes, Lieutenant. If you can lay cover for me once the truck goes up, I should be able to get in and out in about three minutes. I'll need help unrolling the wire."

"William can do that. The rest of the boys lay cover fire for the truck team, while Harvey waits to take aim with the bazooka."

All of this distribution of roles to play is making my head spin! This is a complicated mission we're on! As long as I can stay with William, I'll be fine.

It is awfully impressive that once a plan gets laid out, everyone has a job to do. They're working as a team, with each boy counting on the others to get in there and do what they're supposed to do. I feel proud to be part of such a team and wag my tail to show it.

My wagging tail attracts William's attention.

"Ah, Lieutenant Sir? Can I entrust Barney to your care, Sir? I'd rather he stays near yourself and Harvey, Sir. I wouldn't want him to get lost in the confusion on the bridge."

What's this? William wants me to stay behind?

I sit tall and stop wagging my tail but lean my side into William's legs, reminding him to take me with him.

He squats down in front of me. "Barney old boy, you've got to stay with the Lieutenant and Harvey. They'll need you to be their eyes and ears behind their position. Imagine if some Nazi soldiers come up from behind while Harvey's aiming at the truck on the bridge. This could go wrong for all of us. You understand Barney? You stay."

I sit down near the Lieutenant's feet.

I don't want to be at the Lieutenant's feet. I stand up.

Then I remember my orders and sit back down.

But I can't help myself. I stand back up and circle the Lieutenant's legs, before sitting down once again. I'm nervous.

The boys are nervous too. I can feel their nerves, and smell the sweat break out under the collars of their uniforms like it does when they're worried. I don't like it when they're worried. William is worried.

I stand up. I sit down. I stand up again. I sit down again.

The truck loads up with eight boys. The Lieutenant, myself and the rest of the paratroopers, including Harvey-bazooka take cover from a spot within range and with an excellent view of the road leading to the bridge.

The truck starts off down the road, picking up speed.

Suddenly, gun shots ring out at the truck from windows in the buildings lining the street!

"Oh no! Jerry has seen it's our boys in the truck! The Germans are shooting at them!" whispers the Lieutenant in a very upset sort of whisper.

I jump to my feet and begin to bark.

Ryan bends down to grab my nose and holds my mouth shut. He traps me in his arms as I struggle to break free.

William is in danger!

"Hush, boy! Barney! Calm down!" He tries to comfort me but I can feel he's just as scared as I am.

As the truck reaches the bridge it slams on its brakes, and all eight boys jump out. Four head off in one direction. William, Colum and the other two run off in the opposite direction, crossing the rest of the bridge. Bullets are whizzing all around them.

As soon as everyone is clear of the vehicle, Harvey squats to the ground and raises his bazooka rocket launcher to his shoulder. He's aiming and talking to himself at the same time. "Stay steady. Keep running boys, go, go go!"

The Lieutenant whispers "Fire!"

A terrible noise and a thud ring out as Harvey is knocked backwards onto his bottom. The explosion follows and the truck bursts into flames.

The rest of our boys open fire with their tommy-guns on the windows of the buildings lining the street. Some of the windows have German soldiers firing from behind the curtains, but no one can really tell which ones do and which ones don't.

The noise is deafening, glass is flying everywhere but I have all my attention trained on William. I'm standing, straining against my collar, but Ryan is holding on tight with both hands.

William's sliding down the embankment of the river, following Colum.

They're slipping the explosive charge in the struts holding the bridge on its support legs.

They're hooking the wires to the detonator.

They're climbing back up the embankment. William is unrolling the wire as they go.

Colum reaches the top first and turns around to haul William up by the back of his jacket.

Colum is running down the road in the opposite direction from the burning truck.

William is walking quickly backwards, unrolling the wire as he goes.

There are bullets whizzing and men shouting in German, and in French, and in English. Smoke billows from the burning truck.

William trips and falls. The plunger on the detonator goes off at the same time. A huge explosion causes the bridge to shake. A big hole appears in the road and the burning truck falls slowly into the river.

I can't see William through the smoke. I give in to my fear with a frenzied fit of barking. My body is pulling so hard against my collar that the buckle breaks and I fall forward before taking off at a run towards the last spot I saw

William. My nose is guiding me through the smoke and confusion.

Sun-warmed field grass and toasted bread? William, where are you?

I'm barreling down the road, before plummeting down the embankment. Giving it no thought but moving only by instinct, I leap into the river and swim past the sinking truck.

Sun-warmed field grass and toasted bread?

The current is strong with the early summer rains. I'm carried down river, off my target, but keep paddling as hard as I can, my nose above water, sniffing for sun-warmed field grass and toasted bread.

After what seems a very long swim, I reach the opposite bank. When I haul my back legs onto firm ground, I stand and give a quick shake of my fur to get rid of some of the water. It will slow me down if I'm soaked through.

I can hear Ryan shouting my name, but I simply cannot obey him. Every fiber of my being is driving me to find William.

My forelegs are pounding as I bound up the incline of the slippery grass embankment. So many smells! Explosives and gun powder and gasoline. River water and fish and wet weeds. And finally, sun-warmed field grass and toasted bread… and blood. Warm, fresh, human blood.

Bounding through the smoke, I'm focusing my nose on the good smell and the bad, because I already know they're linked. Just ahead of me, I spot William collapsed on the road. He's clutching his right arm between his knees and groaning in pain.

I stand over top of him, front legs on one side and back legs on the other side. I stand barking, calling out to anyone who'll come and help us, because I know that William needs a kind of assistance that I cannot give him.

Every minute or two, I back up and lick him all over the face to let him know I'm here to help, then take up my guard position once again - barking as loud as I can, while protecting him from any predator who could take advantage of him while he cannot defend himself.

It feels as though time stands still. William is bleeding from his right wrist so much that I fear for his life. He is becoming weaker and weaker. I continue barking and calling, hoping Colum, or Edward or Harry or any of the other boys will hear me and come rescue William.

Suddenly, I can hear a motor cycle engine roaring. It's the jack-rabbit, driven by Edward. George, the medic is hanging on the back.

They both jump off and hit the dirt next to William. I'm delighted to see them and run circles around the group, elated that William will get the help he needs.

Edward and George load William onto the back seat of the jack rabbit and take off. I'm running along behind as fast as I can, but cannot keep up. I can smell the sun-warmed grass and toasted bread moving away from me.

Behind us on the road I can hear another vehicle pursuing. I look over my shoulder and see another motorcycle, this one with a sidecar. It's driven by a German with a helmet and there's an officer riding in the sidecar. He pulls out a pistol and begins shooting at us. At me!

My feet are pulled from beneath me and I tumble head-over tail in the dirt. A sharp pain, dirt on my tongue, a cloud of dust and I can no longer smell sun-warmed field grass or toasted bread.

I can smell blood again, but this time it's mine.

****

My audience has fallen silent. The puppies are looking at their feet, mouths open, stunned into unusual quiet.

"Hey kids! I'm fine! I'm here telling the story, aren't I?" Thumping my tail, I rouse them from their thoughts.

"Who came to save you, Grand-Dog?" one quiet pup asks.

"Why, you haven't guessed by now?" I lift my nose in the direction of the porch where a rocking chair is slowly moving back and forth, driven by the lazy foot of a man holding a newspaper with one hand. "Take a deep breath."

"I smell sun-warmed field grass and toasted bread, Grand-Dog!"

"Well, of course you do. I need a nap now, after all this story telling. If you'll excuse an old dog like me?"

I get up and amble over towards the porch, limp up the steps and lie down at the left side of the rocking chair. The left hand reaches down and rubs my ears.

"Hallo, old boy! How's my old Barney, today?" William asks.

I lick his hand and then drop my nose onto my front paws, sticking my bad leg out to one side.

He knows I'll always be just fine, as long as we stay together.

The End

"Tails of War" is a collection of stories based on the Dickin Medal of Honor, attributed to some of the animals who assisted the war effort. With the publication of Barney, the collection has a story about each of the four different species of animals honored to date: cats, dogs, horses and carrier pigeons.

As I combed through the different stories of the medal of honor recipients, I decided to group together details of different dog related events in order to tell the story of a single fictitious dog, meaning that you won't find a dog named Barney on the list. This is the beauty of historical fiction. And being a Grandmother myself, I let the dog narrate his story to his own grandkids.

While visiting the Pegasus Bridge Museum in Normandy, I saw a photo of a paratrooper dog and wondered what the dog was thinking about that day. Honestly, why would he jump out of an airplane? Fascinating anecdotes about training dogs to leap after steaks filled in missing details. And while I'm not personally tempted to leap into free-fall, I do understand loving steak.

My heartfelt thanks once again go out to my eagle-eyed proofreaders in both French and English, notably: Patrick, Tanya, Martine, Jeff and Kathy and every other "test-reader". It must be terribly annoying as I'm a notoriously bad typist.

A special thanks to Abigail Boutier, who spent agonizing days translating Barney into French for me. How fun is it to have a daughter who can do that thing you hate most? And a fine, conscientious job she did. Kudos to my girl!

I spent a lot of time observing dogs and particularly watching every single border-collie herding video available on the internet.

I particularly loved the one where the sheep wear little lights on their backs and make illuminated shapes on the hillside. These dogs are beyond brilliant. Especially our Barney, who jumps into the hell of WWII Normandy with one of many groups of British paratroopers who were assigned the eastern end of the D-Day invasion beach zone.

The jobs allotted to these different 'sticks' of paratroopers involved a multitude of tasks, all aiming to hinder the German response to the nautical invasion. Largely, all of the Allied paratroopers arrived in the night-time hours preceding the dawn invasion, making their job that much more complicated. Regrouping men scattered over many square miles using herding dogs is more than clever. The Americans used a metal clicker.

In this story, Barney's group was set the task of blowing up a bridge on an east-west road through a town which could be used for German reinforcement troop movement. This sabotage action was crucial, as the Allies had enough opposition on the beaches without additional players being thrown onto the field of action. To the best of my knowledge, there is no town named Petitville in this area. However, the town of Troarn was the target of a successful bridge blowing-up scheme somewhat similar to the events leading to both Barney and William being seriously wounded.

I know a certain percentage of frustrated readers will be shouting questions at me: "How did Barney escape the German officers who shot him? How did William survive? What happened next?" Feel free to use your own imagination to fill in those details and ask your young people to find their own creative answers to those questions. It isn't always necessary for an author to tie up every single thread to get the big picture.

Suffice it to say, Barney, William and the other 156,000 Allied troops did their duty on D-Day and in the many months following through to V.E. day on May 8th, 1945.

Our world is a much better place because of their courage.